Bruce Nauman, **Window or Wall Sign**, 1967

Kröller-Müller Museum

Bart van der Leck, **Affiche Batavier-Line**, 1916

Huize ten Vijver

Anton Kröller, 1862-1941   Helene Kröller-Müller, 1869-1939   H.P. Bremmer, 1871-1956

History

The Kröller-Müller Museum is a modern art museum, situated in Holland's largest nature reserve. It owes its name and its exceptional collection to Mr. and Mrs. Kröller-Müller. Helene Müller was born in 1869 in Horst, near the German city of Essen. Anton Kröller was born in Rotterdam in 1862. Helene's father owned a shipping and trading company in Düsseldorf. He set up a branch in Rotterdam, where Anton's brother Willem became a partner in the firm, which was henceforth known as Müller & Co. Anton met Helene while he was working as a trainee for the company in Düsseldorf. They married in 1888; a year later Anton became the director of the company, his father-in-law having died unexpectedly and his brother having contracted a serious illness. Under Anton's leadership the firm expanded into a worldwide concern. In 1900 the head office was relocated in large premises on Lange Voorhout in The Hague. The Kröller-Müllers moved into the stately 'Huize ten Vijver' in the nearby coastal town of Scheveningen. It is here that Helene embarked on her collection in 1907.

The first purchases

Mrs. Kröller-Müller's interest in and love of art were stimulated by classes given by the art critic and teacher H.P. Bremmer. In the winter of 1906-1907 she, her husband and daughter attended an art appreciation course which Bremmer held in his home on Sundays. Later Bremmer gave these

Paul Gabriël, **Il vient de loin**, ca.1887

Vincent van Gogh, **Edge of a Wood**, 1883

Vincent van Gogh, **Sunflowers**, 1887

Vincent van Gogh, **The Sower** (after Millet), 1889

lessons in the Kröller residence. He became Mrs. Kröller-Müller's principal advisor on acquisitions for her collection. During these early years, in addition to seventeenth-century art, she bought more modern works dating from the latter half of the nineteenth century. One of Helene Kröller-Müller's first purchases was a picture painted in 1887 by the Dutch artist Paul Gabriel. In 1908 she began to collect paintings and drawings by Vincent van Gogh. **Edge of a Wood** was the very first Van Gogh in her collection. It was followed by **Sunflowers** and **The Sower** (after Millet). These were the first of the 272 Van Goghs which were to form the nucleus of her collection.

Peter Behrens, **Model for Ellenwoude**, 1912

6

H.P. Berlage, **Design for St.Hubertus**, 1916

H.P. Berlage, **St.Hubertus** and interior, 1919

The history of the building

Mrs. Kröller-Müller had always envisaged the ideal setting for her collection: a kind of museum-house which would be both a home and the proper setting for her collection. In order to realize her vision she collaborated with a number of architects over the ensuing decades. In 1910 the Kröllers purchased 'Ellenwoude', a country estate in Wassenaar, as a site for their building. Peter Behrens (1868-1940) of Germany was the first architect to submit plans for the museum-house. A full-scale wood and canvas model was even constructed and mounted on rails so as to determine the best place for the building in the landscape. However, Behrens' design was rejected. The Kröllers then recruited Ludwig Mies van der Rohe (1886-1969), a pupil of Behrens, and H.P. Berlage (1856-1934). A full-scale model was

made of Mies van der Rohe's design too; not only was this model photographed but a detailed perspective drawing of it was also made. Even so, the plans of both architects were turned down, perhaps because of the growing realization that the Wassenaar location was not so suitable after all.

In the meantime Anton Kröller had purchased large areas of land in the Veluwe region on which to hunt and ride. The Hoge Veluwe offered new perspectives for a museum-house. In 1916 Berlage submitted his design. He was also commissioned to build a hunting lodge on the estate (Jachthuis Sint Hubertus). Berlage was responsible for the entire interior design of the lodge as well.

Henry van de Velde, **Design for the large museum**, 1920

The official opening of the 'Temporary' Museum

Lange Voorhout, interior

Berlage, who had worked for Müller & Co. for six years, resigned in 1919. That same year the Belgian architect Henry van de Velde (1863-1957) was invited to design a new museum. He planned a large building, which he worked out in minute detail. Construction started in 1920. In 1921, however, an economic crisis brought work to a halt.

The foundations of the building still lie at the foot of 'Franse Berg' ('French Hill') as a reminder of Helene Kröller-Müller's ambitious plans.

A large part of her collection remained in the house on Lange Voorhout in The Hague, where it could be viewed on appointment. In 1928 the Kröller-Müllers set up a foundation for the collection. Later, in 1935, it was presented to the Nation. In exchange, a small and what was supposed to be a temporary museum was built; it, too, was designed by Henry van de Velde.

The final result of Helene Kröller's ambitious plans was a small, sober building with a severe, closed character. Inspired by the works in the collection, Van de Velde opted for a symmetrical, lucid structure. The museum was opened on July 13 1938. It had taken 27 years to realize Helene Kröller-Müller's vision: her private collection was now public!

Mrs. Kröller-Müller once characterized her collection as follows: 'Assembled for the benefit

and pleasure of the community, this collection is intended to illustrate the development of both the individual modern artist and the art of our times in general.'

In the early fifties Henry van de Velde was asked to add a sculpture gallery to the museum. He designed a tall-windowed room which established a connection with the building's natural surroundings. The fundamental idea of relating art and nature was also behind the subsequent sculpture garden (1961), the Rietveld pavilion (1965), the sculpture park and sculpture wood (1988). In 2002 the complex of sculpture garden, park and wood was given back its original name of "sculpture garden".

The relationship between art and nature also featured prominently in the new museum building designed between 1870 and 1977 by the Dutch architect Wim Quist (b. 1930).

The Rietveld Pavilion

The Rietveld Pavilion was designed in 1955 by Gerrit Rietveld (1888-1964) for the presentation of small sculptures in an open-air exhibition in Sonsbeek Park, Arnhem. In 1965 this severe, transparent structure was rebuilt in the museum's sculpture garden on a site selected by Rietveld. Around a central space measuring twelve by twelve metres he grouped three galleries, each three metres wide. The walls enclosing the central space are not painted in Rietveld's usual primary colours, but are pale pink, pale yellow and pale blue. The materials used for the construction are distinctly visible on the outside: metal U-girders for the skeleton, concrete stone for the walls and glass for the galleries.

A characteristic feature is the gradual transition from inside to outside, from partially closed to open space. The sculptures on show in the pavilion are both part of the nature outside and partly sheltered from it.

Wim Quist, New wing of the museum, 1970-77

Large sculpture room with exhibition Gerrit van Bakel in 1992

The old and new tracts of the museum differ considerably in appearance, and to a certain extent in their function too. In contrast to Henry van de Velde's closed, compact museum, Wim Quist (b. 1930) designed an elongated, asymmetrical building with a distinctly open character. The museum's two sections house different collections. Most of the paintings from the Kröller-Müller collection are in the old building. In the new extension, with its large, almost square rooms, modern sculptures and sculptors' drawings. Temporary exhibitions of 20th and 21st-century art are also held here.

Wim Quist, **exhibition room**

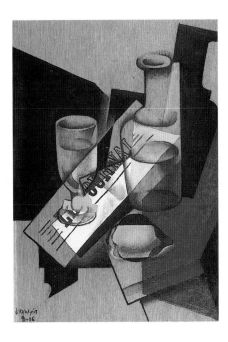

Juan Gris, **Still Life with Water-Bottle and Lemon**, 1916

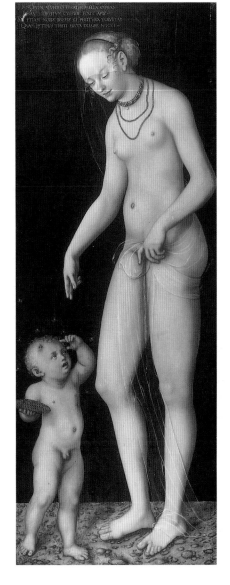

Lucas Cranach the Elder, **Venus with Cupid Stealing Honey**, after 1537

The painting collection

In 1907 Helene Kröller-Müller embarked on her collection which gradually came to contain both old master paintings of the sixteenth and seventeenth centuries and relatively modern art dating from the second half of the nineteenth century. First and foremost, though, the pictures she collected had just left the artists' studios.

Helene Kröller-Müller

13

Floris van Schooten, **Breakfast Piece**, n.d.

Floris van Schooten (before 1612 – after 1655)

Floris van Schooten is one of the best-known painters of what are known as 'ontbijtjes', or 'breakfast pieces': still lifes displaying a rich variety of food and tableware. In the fifteenth and sixteenth centuries such objects were depicted in religious representations or portraits. In the seventeenth century, however, the still life developed into an independent genre with religious and symbolic undertones. Bread and wine usually refer to the Eucharist; meat and cheese are reminders of the brevity of life on earth. All the objects in this little painting are rendered in a painstakingly accurate and realistic manner. Floris van Schooten uses the device of a high horizon, with the attributes facing the beholder. He accentuates this with a pronounced light and dark contrast and by having the some of the objects project beyond the edge of the table. The profusion displayed here reflects the prosperity enjoyed by the Netherlands in the seventeenth century because of the country's trade with the Far East. The Chinese plate and the exotic fruit are references to this prosperity.

Jean Baptiste Camille Corot, **View of Soissons**, 1833

Henri Fantin Latour, **Portrait of Eva Callimaki Cartagi**, 1881

Helene Kröllers ideas about art

According to Mrs. Kröller, there had always been two movements in every period of art. She called them Realism and Idealism. Realists, she contended, were primarily concerned with recording perceptible reality.
Idealists, on the other hand, were artists of the idea: less preoccupied by **what** they actually saw than by **how** they saw it.
To illustrate this notion, here is a quotation from Mrs. Kröller's book 'Beschouwingen over problemen in de ontwikkeling der moderne

schilderkunst' ('Observations on problems in the development of modern painting'), of 1925.

'My point of departure will be the **Realism** of 1870-1890, which formed such a healthy basis for a regular development of art into the **Idealism** of our own time. For each phase of this development a name, an 'ism', has established itself (...).
Our point of departure will be **Modern Realism**, which dissolved into **Impressionism**. It expanded in **Neo-Impressionism** and gained depth in

Isaäc Israëls, **Café-Chantant in the Nes**, c. 1893

George Hendrik Breitner, **Gust of Wind**, c. 1890

Charles François Daubigny, **Young Corn**, n.d.

Jean-François Millet, **Woman Baking Bread**, 1854

Pointillism, thereby deliberately veering towards the art of the idea, **Idealism**. To this **Cubism** also belongs, with its expressions of extreme abstraction (...). For art is always seeking and yearning, art never stands still.'

The movements represented in the Kröller-Müller museum collection reflect that vision. Realism, for instance, can be seen in the works of nineteenth-century painters such as Courbet, Corot, Daubigny, Fantin Latour and Millet. These artists strongly influenced Dutch painters of their generation: Jongkind and Gabriel, for example, and in particular the painters of the 'Amsterdam School', including Israëls and Breitner.
Painters of the late nineteenth and early twentieth century such as Redon, Seurat, Cézanne, Picasso, Braque, Gris, Léger, Van der Leck, Van Doesburg and Mondrian, were regarded by Mrs. Kröller as 'Painters of the Idea'. Nowadays they are qualified as representatives of Symbolism, Cubism and De Stijl.

Henri Fantin Latour, **Still Life**, 1866

Edouard Manet, **Portrait of a Man**, 1860

Realism

Gustave Courbet, **Portrait of Madame Jolicler**, c. 1873

Realism appeared in France as a reaction to
Academic art. For a long time painting had been
dominated by the Academy, which contended that
allegorical representations, historical events and
biblical scenes were the only worthwhile subjects.
Courbet became Realism's leading spokesman.
In 1861 he wrote: 'Painting is essentially very
concrete and can only exist in the depiction of
things that actually exist.'
Courbet and kindred spirits were interested
primarily in reality; as realistically as possible
they wanted to paint ordinary people, their habits
and their milieu, as an image of their own time.

Camille Pissarro, **The Rainbow**, 1877

Impressionism

Pierre Auguste Renoir, **The Café**, c. 1876

Mrs. Kröller regarded the Impressionist painters
Monet, Pissarro, Signac, Renoir and Sisley as
Realists too. The Impressionists left their studios
to paint in the open air. Using a light palette, they
endeavoured to record immediate impressions:
changing light, colours and atmosphere. Their
shapes do not have solid outlines, but are built up
with rapidly applied dabs of paint.
At first the Impressionists were chiefly interested
in the landscape and the way it changes under the
influence of the seasons. Later they turned their
attention to sophisticated forms of entertainment
and to a new phenomenon: the leisure activities
of the bourgeoisie.

18

Paul Gaugain, **The Edge of the Wood**, 1885

Claude Monet, **The Painter's Boat**, c. 1874

Georges Seurat (1859 – 1891)

The Impressionists discovered the effect of colour during the act of painting; Seurat developed and systematized their method. Seurat reduced their dabs of colour to a dot, or point. He limited himself to seven hues: yellow, orange, red, green, blue, indigo and purple - the colours of the rainbow, the colours of which light is composed. Seurat placed dots of these unmixed colours so close together that when seen from a distance they blend optically into forms and colours.
Le Chahut is dominated by the verve of Parisian night-life; the tone is light, the colours are warm. The composition, with its upward movement of parallel lines, emphasizes the cheerful mood. Everything in this painting is studied and deliberate. The people and objects are distinctly separate and shown in profile; only the bass-player in the foreground is seen from the rear. The painting does not create an illusion of space or depth; the effect is that of a freeze-frame. In Seurat's work Mrs. Kröller-Müller saw a 'veering towards the art of the idea, idealism.'

Paul Cézanne, **Road Along the Lake**, 1885-90

Paul Cézanne (1839 – 1906)

Like Seurat, Cézanne developed Impressionism still further. His awareness of the vagaries of nature - the changing colours, light, shade and atmosphere - did not however lead to a further disintegration of colour or to more undefined forms. On the contrary, they stimulated Cézanne to search for structure. Instead of registering space, shapes and colours like the Impressionists, Cézanne arranges, systematizes and constructs them. He analyses the forms of nature, reducing them to the cylinder, cone and sphere. Patiently and with restraint, he searches for a harmony of form and colour: each stroke is a constructional element in his pictorial architecture. In **Road Along the Lake** the brushstrokes are placed systematically in three directions: vertical, horizontal and diagonal. Cézanne does not paint lines or volumes, but gradations of colour; the forms are built up in different shades of ochre, green, grey and blue. The shadow on the path, the edge of the wood behind the houses and the mountain ridge create a rhythm of horizontal bands. The trees in the foreground, severely vertical, close off the picture and at the same time open up a prospect, as if through a gate, leading the eye along the road towards the lake.

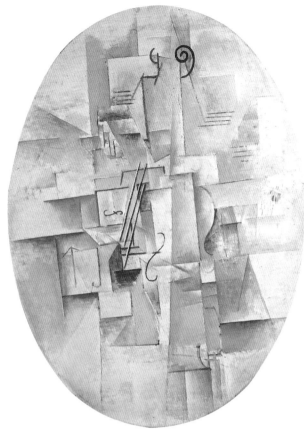

Georges Braque, **Still Life in Diamond Shape**, 1917

Pablo Picasso, **The Violin**, 1911-12

Cubism

Cubism, originated by Picasso (1881-1973) and Braque (1882-1963), developed at the beginning of the century. The ideas of Seurat and Cézanne were an important impulse, but so was African art, which was attracting great attention in France at the time. Picasso and Braque sought a radical innovation of art. The painted picture had long been a rendering of reality, constructed according to the rules of central perspective like a window on the world.

Picasso and Braque went a step further than Seurat and Cézanne, treating the canvas as a flat surface and banishing all illusion of depth. The centre of the canvas is the starting point for their compositions. Objects are shown simultaneously from different angles in one and the same painting. The forms consist of geometrical planes; the name 'Cubist' derives from these angular shapes. Colour is avoided, reduced to ochres and greys. A kind of optical structure does however result from the contrast between light and dark paint. In this structure, all the forms face the beholder. In 1912 Picasso and Braque finally liberated painting from its tradition. Depicting materials

Juan Gris, **Still Life with Guitar**, 1915

Fernand Léger, **The Typographer**, 1919

was no longer a matter of painting, but of
introducing the actual materials - scraps of
newspaper, wallpaper, rope and sand.
These collage techniques heralded a vast
expansion of artistic means.
Cubism had far-reaching consequences for the
development of both the painting and sculpture
of the twentieth century.

Piet Mondrian, **The Sea near Domburg**, n.d.

Piet Mondrian, **Composition in Line and Colour**, c. 1912

Mondriaan, Van der Leck and De Stijl

Helene Kröller-Müller regarded Cubism and De Stijl as 'idealistic art'. De Stijl was the title of an art periodical edited by Van Doesburg (1883-1931); the first number appeared in 1917. Not only artists but also architects and designers aired their ideas in this publication, which due to Theo van Doesburg's contacts soon acquired an international character. The 'Stijl' artists shunned representation and resorted chiefly to elementary means: the straight line, the three primary colours (red, yellow and blue) and the non-colours (white, grey and black). In the beginning Mondrian (1872-1944) and Van der Leck 1876-1958) collaborated on the magazine.

Piet Mondrian started off as a naturalistic painter, chiefly of traditional, dark landscapes. He later experimented with other colours and formal reduction. This simplification and the increasing intensity of his colours invest his paintings of the lighthouse at Westkapelle and the beach and dunes of Walcheren with an expressionistic, even monumental character.

In 1911 Mondrian moved to Paris, where he fell under the spell of the Cubists and was influenced by Picasso and Braque. During this cubist period he limited his palette to a few muted hues, - ochre and grey at first, later pastel shades too.

He reduced his forms more and more into planes,

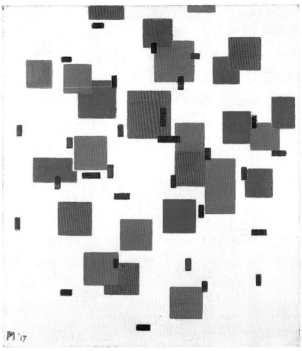

Piet Mondrian, **Composition no. 10** (Pier and Ocean), 1915

Piet Mondrian, **Composition in Colour A**, 1917

building up his compositions from the centre of the canvas, as in **Composition in Line and Colour**. In 1914 Mondrian returned to Holland, where the war forced him to stay until 1919.

With his **Composition no. 10 (Pier and Ocean**, Mondrian's most important work of this period), he took a radical step towards abstraction. In this painting a motif from nature, waves and the way they are broken by the pier, is reduced to a rhythmic pattern of horizontal and vertical lines inside a horizontal oval.

His return to Paris in 1919 heralded a new period in which his paintings were characterised by horizontal and vertical black lines connecting and separating planes of white or primary colours. 'Neoplasticism' was Mondrian's name for this attempt to harmonise opposites such as logic and emotion, spiritual and material, male and female. He spent the rest of his life in search of that future harmony, regarding his paintings as harbingers or blueprints.

Bart van der Leck, **The Tempest**, 1916

Bart van der Leck started off as a stained-glass artist in Utrecht. He later attended the Rijksacademie in Amsterdam to become a painter.

Throughout his life he was fascinated by the relationship between painting, architecture and the decorative arts. For some time before joining De Stijl, and motivated by a strong sense of social commitment, he attempted to divest the human figure of its individual characteristics, simplifying and stylizing them in order to emphasize their universal character. In this manner he hoped to make his art accessible to a large public.

In 1914 Mrs. Kröller-Müller sent him to North Africa, where he made drawings of the ore-mining area belonging to the firm of Kröller-Müller & Co. These drawings became the point of departure for his later work. In 1916 he became the first to use the primary colours and black and white in his paintings **Havenarbeid** (Dockworkers) and **De Storm** (The Tempest). He met Mondrian that year; their contact stimulated him to render his subject even more abstract, as demonstrated by his **Composition 1917 no. 4 (Leaving the Factory)**. For a while in 1918 he made completely abstract works, such as **Composition 1918 no. 4**.

Later, though, he returned to representation, albeit in a strongly abstract form. His themes were no longer inspired by social commitment

Bart van der Leck, **Composition 1918 no. 4**

Bart van der Leck, **Composition 1917 no. 4** (Leaving the factory)

Theo van Doesburg, **Geometrical Composition**, 1916

but focused more on his personal environment: family, animals, flowers.

'White' remained an important element in his work, the white background on which planes of colour are arranged without touching.

In addition to paintings and drawings Bart van der Leck designed a large number of murals, interiors, tiles and carpets.

The Kröller-Müller Museum owns 43 of Van der Leck's paintings, 236 drawings and a carpet.

Vincent van Gogh, **Self-Portrait**, 1887

Vincent van Gogh, **Vegetable gardens (Laan van Meerdervoort)**, 1883

Vincent van Gogh, **Binding Sheaves**, 1885

Vincent van Gogh (1853 – 1890)

Vincent van Gogh occupied a special place in Helene Kröller-Müller's life and hence in her collection. She saw him as 'one of the great souls of our modern art, on whom the spirit of the times had no grasp.'
In 1912 she was able to add 35 of his paintings to her collection. Today the museum owns 87 paintings paintings, 183 drawings, 1 etching and 2 lithographs by Van Gogh.
Van Gogh decided to become an artist in 1880 while he was working as a lay preacher among the miners of the Borinage region. This was in 1880. He had spent the previous six years in the employ of Goupil & Co. Art Dealers, working in its Hague, London and Paris branches. Painting and drawing had always fascinated him. In 1872 he started writing to his brother Theo. This unique correspondence is a rich source of information about Vincent's ideas, drawings and paintings.
At first, in Brussels and Etten, his drawings were modelled on Millet's works. Other models came from his immediate surroundings. His first oil sketches were done in 1882 in The Hague, where he took lessons from Mauve.
During this period he drew numerous town views, old men in a home for the aged and his friend Sien and her children. For the next two years he worked in his parents' home in Nuenen.
This proved to be an important period in his life. The harsh and arduous existence of the peasants and weavers around him is the subject of countless drawings and paintings. He also painted a number of landscapes. His best-known painting of this period is **The Potato Eaters**, which Van Gogh said 'reminded [him] of a totally different way of life.'

Vincent van Gogh, **The Potato Eaters**, 1885

Travelling by way of Antwerp he joined his brother Theo in Paris in 1886, where he saw the new impressionist paintings and struck up friendships with Pissarro, Gauguin and Bernard. Within a few months his technique and use of colour underwent a complete change. During his two-year stay in Paris he painted several flower and fruit still lifes, town views and a large number of self-portraits in bright, light colours.

Eventually, however, he decided to live and work in the country and left for Arles, where he fell under the spell of the clear southern light. Many of his most important works were painted here. He had hopes of founding an artists' colony in Arles, but only Gauguin made the journey south. Unfortunately, a dramatic quarrel put an end to their friendship. Although Van Gogh made a rapid recovery from his subsequent serious depression, he sought peace and treatment in the hospital at Saint-Rémy de Provence. Most of his paintings here were of the garden, the view of the cornfield and a few portraits. His brushwork was now fast and direct. The compositions, often based on pronounced diagonals, have a strongly spatial and dynamic character.

Van Gogh was constantly endeavouring to capture the essence of his subjects. Most of the paintings, watercolours and drawings of his last three months in Auvers-sur-Oise reflect the intense feelings evoked by the vast sweep of landscape. Van Gogh not only observed, like the Impressionists, but was also an artist who aspired to express his communion with nature in emotional lines, planes and colours, thereby abandoning the traditional manner of painting.

Vincent van Gogh, **Young girl in a wood**, 1882

'The other study in the wood is of some large
green beech trunks on a stretch of ground
covered with dry sticks, and the little figure of a
girl in white. There was the great difficulty of
keeping it clear, and of getting space between the
trunks standing at different distances - and the
place and relative bulk of those trunks change
with the perspective - to make it so that one can
breath and walk around in it, and to make you
smell the fragrance of the wood.'

Letter to Theo van Gogh
The Hague, August 20, 1882

Vincent van Gogh, **Flowers in a blue vase**, 1887

'And now for what regards what I myself have been doing, I have lacked money for paying models else I had entirely given myself to figure painting. But I have made a series of colour studies in painting, simply flowers, red poppies, blue corn flowers an myosotys, white and rose roses, yellow chrysanthemums, seeking oppositions of blue with orange, red and green, yellow and violet seeking "les tons rompus et neutres" to harmonise brutal extremes. Trying to render intense colour and not a grey harmony.'

Letter to H.M. Livens
Paris, autumn 1886

Vincent van Gogh, **Terrace of a café at night ('Place du Forum')**, 1888

'On the terrace there are the tiny figures of people
drinking. An enormous yellow lantern sheds its
light on the terrace, the house front and the
sidewalk, and even casts a certain brightness on
the pavement of the street, which takes a pinkish
violet tone. The gable-topped fronts of the houses
in a street stretching away under a blue sky
spangled with stars are dark blue or violet and
there is a green tree. Here you have a night
picture without any black in it, done with nothing
but beautiful blue and violet and green, and in
these surroundings the lighted square acquires a
pale sulphur and greenish citron-yellow color.
It amuses me enormously to paint the night right
on the spot.'

Letter to Wil van Gogh
Arles, September 9 and 16, 1888

Vincent van Gogh, **Vineyard 'La vigne verte'**, 1888

'The "Vines" that I have just painted are green, purple and yellow, with violet bunches and branches in black and orange. On the horizon a few blue-grey willows and far, far away the winepress with a red roof and the mauve silhouette of a town in the distance. In the vineyard figures of women with red parasols and other small figures of grape-pickers with their cart. Over it is a blue sky, and the foreground is of gray gravel.'

Letter to Theo
Arles, October 3, 1888

Vincent van Gogh, **Cypresses with two figures**, 1889-90

'The cypresses are always occupying my thoughts,
I should like to make something of them like the
canvases of the sunflowers, because it astonishes
me that they have not yet been done as I see
them. It is as beautiful of line and proportions
as an Egyptian obelisk (...). It is a splash of black
in a sunny landscape, but it is one of the most
interesting black notes, and the most difficult to
hit off exactly that I can imagine.'

Letter to Theo van Gogh
St. Rémy, June 25, 1889

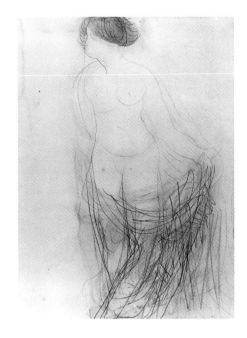

Auguste Rodin, **Female Nude**, n.d.

Auguste Rodin, **Mask of Hanako**, 1908

The sculpture collection

Mrs. Kröller died in 1939. She regarded her collection as a complete entity. This point of view was respected by her successors. Consequently the museum acquired a different character after World War Two. The accent was now on the collection and presentation of modern sculpture and sculptors' drawings. In this manner a new collection was formed which confronts the visitor with the development of sculpture in the Twentieth Century.

Impressionism breathed new life not only into painting, but into sculpture too. The work of Medardo Rosso and Auguste Rodin was of crucial importance. Rodin's **Man with a Broken Nose** (1864) met with disapproval for the same reason as impressionist paintings were rejected: it was regarded as unfinished, little more than a sketch. Rodin was the first sculptor to make an aesthetic principle of the unfinished figure. **Man with a Broken Nose** is not a bust, but a head 'broken off' at the neck.

As for Rosso, the free and lively preliminary studies in clay and wax which had previously served as practice material now acquired the status of autonomous works of art. Both artists investigated the effect of light and shade.

Emile-Antoine Bourdelle, **Large Penelope**, 1912

Wilhelm Lehmbruck, **Standing Female Figure**, 1915

Aristide Maillol, **Sky**, 1939

Their feeling for surface, and their treatment of it
in the material, generated a powerful emotional
charge in their sculpture.
This approach liberated sculpture from its hitherto
decorative and functional character. Rosso and
Rodin had a strong influence on the next
generation of sculptors such as Bourdelle,
Lehmbruck and Maillol.

Auguste Rodin, **Squatting Woman**, 1882

Auguste Rodin (1840 – 1917)

For a long time Rodin earned a living by assisting academic sculptors like Dalou and Carpeaux. Under their supervision he worked on facade ornaments and other commissions. **Man with a Broken Nose**, which was rejected by the Salon, dates from this period. After working as an assistant in Brussels for another five years, Rodin went to Italy on a study trip which proved to be of vital importance to him. Studying the sculpture of Michelangelo and Donatello, he discovered the way to liberate himself from the academicism of his own day.

In 1876 he exhibited **The Age of Bronze**. It was so lifelike that he was accused of having cast it directly from a living model. Not until the end of 1877 did his work elicit a favourable response. He received a commission for **The Gates of Hell**, the doors of the future Musée des Arts Décoratifs in Paris. He was to spend the rest of his life on this work, which was unfinished at his death. In the meantime he presented sections of the doors as autonomous works. **Squatting Woman** ('La Luxure'), for instance, also occurs in a modified form in the tympanum above the door. Many of the formal problems which preoccupied Rodin during this period are addressed in this sculpture: the degree to which equilibrium can be achieved in an extreme pose, the limits to which muscles can be stretched and within which powerful emotions can be convincingly depicted. The outline of **Squatting Woman** is virtually closed, despite the extremely complex positions of the various parts of the body. Due to the intricate patterns of light and shade on the surface and the figure's impassioned attitude, **La Luxure** (lust) has an powerfully expressive impact.

Medardo Rosso, **Child in the Sun**, 1892

Medardo Rosso (1858 – 1928)

In his native land, Italy, where sculpture still clung to the neo-classical tradition, Rosso had always had his own place. Even his very first sculptures are modelled in an 'impressionist' manner. He endeavoured to express the mobility of light and shade in works whose overall expression is more important than the separate parts. In particular the portrayal of little children, whose facial features are still undeveloped, suggested to Rosso a means of 'dissolving' form into a play of light and shade. He preferred to work in the pliable materials clay and wax, and worked his bronzes until their surfaces conveyed the same improvized impression. In 1898 - by which time he was living in Paris - Rodin's **Balzac** sparked off a bitter and fruitless quarrel between the two artists as to which of them had introduced Impressionism to sculpture. The dispute had an adverse effect on Rosso's further career, for Rodin reigned supreme in France by this time. Only the Futurists recognized the value of his work, and Rosso gradually slipped into oblivion. The latter half of the 20th century saw a revival of appreciation for the innovative and radical aspect of his work.

Umberto Boccioni, **Unique Forms of Continuity in Space**, 1913

Chaim Jacob Lipchitz, **Standing Figure**, 1915

Boccioni, Lipchitz and Gonzalez

The development of cubist painting opened up new perspectives for sculpture too. In the first decades of the 20th century sculptors sought simplification, movement and structure, employing a variety of means in their efforts to abandon the direct imitation of reality.
The sculpture became a dynamic play of geometric forms and planes.

The work of Boccioni (1882-1916) and Lipchitz (1891-1973) exemplifies this innovative development. Not only does Boccioni's **Unique Forms of Continuity in Space** suggest a series of freeze-frames of a body in motion, it also conveys an impression of continuous, flowing movement. This is an image of speed, the speed of the figure surging forward to conquer space.

The Futurists - the group of Italian artists to whom Boccioni belonged - admired the latest technical developments which enabled people to experience the sensation of speed and dynamic force: the automobile, the train, the aeroplane. Their 'Futurist Manifesto' (1909) states that "a racing car is much more beautiful than 'The Victory of Samothrace'", the famous Greek sculpture in the Louvre.

The sculptors Gonzalez, Zadkine and Lipchitz, who lived in France, had a different approach to Cubism. Lipchitz saw it as a means of escape from the naturalistic depiction of reality, and started to base his works on a pre-planned geometrical conception. For a long time his sculpture was dominated by symmetry, alternating straight lines

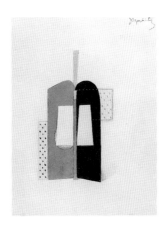

Chaim Jacob Lipchitz, **Study for Sculpture**, 1915

Chaim Jacob Lipchitz, **Song of the Vowels**, 1930-31

Julio Gonzalez, **Head with Gaping Mouth**, n.d.

Julio Gonzalez, **Prayer**, 1932

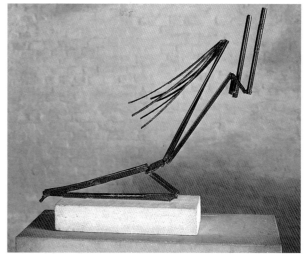

and curves and a frontal treatment of the subject. By 1915 his work had become so abstract in his own opinion that he destroyed most of it in a moment of crisis. Henceforth his sculptures were characterized by the tension between figuration and abstraction. Around 1920 his work became symbiotic - coalescences of two or more separate entities. In **Song of the Vowels**, for instance, the harp and the women playing it fuse into a single, powerful form which exhibits a harmonious balance of mass and space.

Gonzalez (1875-1942) started to produce welded iron sculptures in 1927. This was the first time in the history of sculpture that an artist had employed industrial materials and techniques. Gonzalez' job at the Renault car factory had

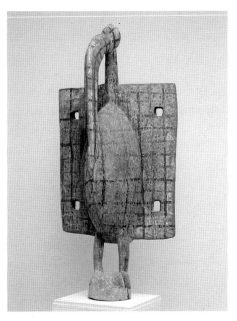

Hornbill, Ivory Coast, n.d.

Top part of a mask, Sudan, n.d.

Not-Western Art

familiarized him with this approach. Space is
crucial to Gonzalez' work: the void as an artistic
element. He himself put it as follows: 'to design
and draw in space with new means, to make use
of that space and work with it as if it were a new
material.' As well as open sculptures with a
graphic character, Gonzalez welded and forged
masks which often have a frightening appearance,
their forms strongly reminiscent of African
sculpture.

Around the turn of the century many artists
became interested in the art of other cultures,
notably African art.
African masks, figures and utensils often have
strongly stylized forms in which symmetry and
simplification result in a high degree of
abstraction. It was chiefly this exotic, powerful
idiom, but also the magical character of these
objects, that exerted a direct influence on artists.
The museum's small collection of non-western art
was originally Mrs. Kröller's work. She collected
art from different cultures, in accordance with her
philosophy that Realism and Idealism (see p.15)
were not bound to a particular period or culture.
Chinese pottery, Japanese silk paintings, Egyptian
statuary and Khmer figures were of special

Man and Woman, Cambodia, 12th century

Large split drum, New Hebrides, 19th century

Grave stele of the scribe Ramessu, Egypt, c. 1400 B.C.

interest to her. As the years passed, additions were made to this collection of non-western Art, generally in the form of gifts; they include African masks, small items of pre-Columbian sculpture, Inuit steatite figures from Canada and a slit drum from Oceania.

Henry Moore, **Two-Piece Reclining Figure II**, 1960

Moore and Hepworth

Henry Moore, **Reclining Figures**, 1934

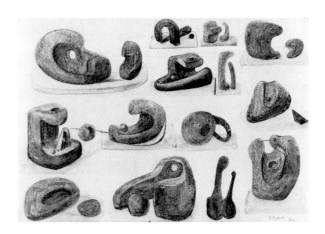

Non-western cultures were an important source of inspiration to a growing number of artists. They influenced not only the idiom but also the choice of material. Carving the wood or stone directly, artists sought to reveal the original structure of the material. The closed volume was opened up, and space penetrated the sculpture. This phenomenon is a prominent feature of the work of the postwar generation of British sculptors, of whom Henry Moore (1898-1986) and Barbara Hepworth (1903-1975) are the leading exponents. The young Henry Moore was strongly influenced by pre-Columbian objects in the British

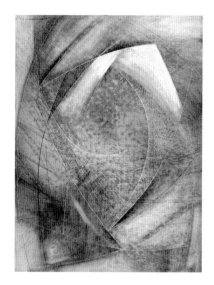

Barbara Hepworth, **Marble form** (Mycenea), 1959

Barbara Hepworth, **Sphere with Inner Form**, 1963

Museum. He approached abstraction most closely in the years before the war, when he made an intensive study of the structure of vertebrae, bones and shells. His sculptures, at first angular, rough and 'primitive', gradually became more curved and smooth. The relationship between the closed volume and space is particularly apparent in his monumental reclining figures. He preferred to have his pieces placed in a landscape setting: 'Only in nature the work will be finally completed.' As well as the relationship between sculpture and landscape, Moore explored classical sculptural themes: the head, the reclining figure, the seated figure, the mother and child motif, the family. An important source of inspiration to Barbara Hepworth was the scenery of Cornwall - the sea, hills and valleys. Her abstract sculptures, with their flowing lines and organic transitions, are often reminiscent of natural growth processes. **Sphere with Inner Form** features two themes which are significant throughout Hepworth's œuvre: a small form resting in a large, enveloping form, and the opening through which light can penetrate to the heart of the volume.

Mark Di Suvero, **K-Piece**, 1972

Di Suvero, Oldenburg and Christo

In Europe in the 1950s and 1960s landscape and the human figure were still the most important sculptural themes. In American sculpture, by contrast, the focus was no longer on the human figure but on construction. Modern techniques like welding, torchcutting and riveting, and industrial materials such as steel, aluminium and plastics gave rise to huge open works no longer set on plinths, but standing out like powerful signs in their surroundings. Di Suvero (1933), for instance, abandons human dimensions. His sculptures always consist of heavy wooden beams or steel girders with which he tries to establish an equilibrium. Because of their size, weight and audacious construction, his pieces can only be placed out of doors.

Claes Oldenburg, **Trowel**, 1971

Kenneth Snelson, **Needle Tower**, 1968

Another group of artists of that period commented on the modern world of advertizing, mass consumption and mass media by lifting ordinary objects out of their context and dubbing them art. Oldenburg (1929), for instance, employs materials alien to the original objects and blows them up to a gigantic scale. Like so many of his pieces, **Trowel**, originally made for the sculpture exhibition held in Sonsbeek Park, Arnhem, in 1971, resulted from a series of casual sketches.
He always makes notes of things he encounters in daily life. The idea of a huge trowel had been on his mind for some time, and when he saw all the molehills in Sonsbeek park it assumed concrete form.

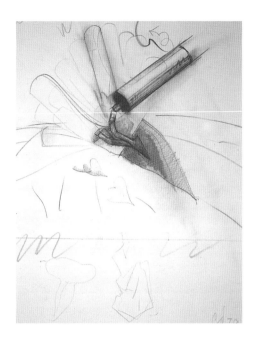

Claes Oldenburg, **Study for Trowel**, 1970

Christo, **Otterlo Mastaba**, 1973

Claes Oldenburg, **Model for Trowel**, 1971

Christo, **Empaquetage**, 1961

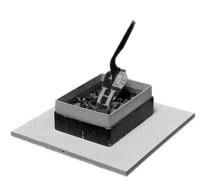

This alienation of everyday objects can also be seen in the work of Christo (1935). In 1972 he had the idea of building an enormous mastaba of oil-drums on the museum parking lot. He also alienates objects by shrouding them in mysterious wrappings.

Robert Morris, **4 Unit Floor Piece**, 1967

Donald Judd, **Untitled**, 1977

Minimal Art

The years 1965/1970 heralded an extremely important phase in American art. The sculpture produced during this period goes by the somewhat vague name of Minimal Art.

Sculpture left its plinth, assumed severe geometrical shape and entered into a relationship with its immediate architectural surroundings. First and foremost, however, sculpture was reduced to a purely material object, with no meaning other than the meaning deduced from perception. The personal 'hand' of the artist is no longer important; the work is often made by someone else.

The Kröller-Müller Museum has a remarkable collection of Minimal Art, with work by Carl Andre (1935), Robert Morris (1931), Donald Judd (1928-

1994), Sol LeWitt (1928) and Dan Flavin (1933-1996). Robert Morris is represented in the collection by, among others, **4 Unit Floor Piece**: four identical pale grey metal elements placed on the floor to form a square. Despite its extreme simplicity, this work dominates the room and seems to float. Donald Judd's six large plywood boxes are also identical and anonymous. It is the movement of the beholder, his changing viewpoint, that brings the work to life. Judd does not want his pieces to stimulate the imagination, but would rather trigger a conscious awareness of 'real objects in real space' in the beholder.

In the sixties Dan Flavin started making sculptures from standard neon tubes of various sizes and colours. One of his pieces, **Quietly, to the Memory**

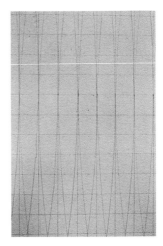

Sol LeWitt, **6 Part Piece**, 1968

Sol LeWitt, **Wall Drawing**, detail, 1972

Dan Flavin, **Quietly, to the memory of Mia Visser**, 1977

of Mia Visser, is fixed to the wall linking the museum cafeteria with the terrace.

Sol LeWitt's work is based on his research into the possibilities of variation in an open and closed cube. He is particularly intrigued by the rules governing serial construction. One of his **Wall Drawings** is a permanent fixture on a wall in the Van de Velde building. The measurements of the wall provided the point of departure for its systematic division into squares and circles.

Carl Andre, **Square Piece**, 1967

Carl Andre, **35 Timber Row**, 1968

Carl Andre, **Henge on Threshold**, 1960

Carl Andre, **43 Roaring Forty**, 1987

Carl Andre (1935)

Carl Andre's work is highly significant for having inspired a totally new vision of sculpture.

His first sculptures of 1958-59 were forms carved in wood and entitled **Ladder**. A year later he was piling identical, unworked blocks of wood into forms held together by their own mass. The series of **Henges** dates from 1960. Both the name and form refer to piling up elements as the oldest and most elementary architectural action (Stonehenge, Woodhenge).

All Andre's pieces consist of identical elements, serially arranged into simple, lucid structures. He produces squares, rows, lines and piles. In many cases the same piece can be arranged in different ways, depending on the room. In this manner various aspects of the piece's surroundings can be related to the work itself. As well as metal plates, nails, pieces of chalk and bricks Andre has always used wood, which he regards as 'the mother of all matter'.

Lying or standing, Andre's work is always closely linked with the ground and the earth.

'My work has no more idea than a tree, or a rock, or a mountain, or an ocean'.

Richard Long, **Stone Line**, 1976

Land Art

Between 1970 and 1980 a new generation turned away from the urban environment, the use of industrial materials and the constructive approach. Instead, they opted for secluded areas and for material at hand. Their sculptures were generally made in remote sites with the aid of naturally occurring elements such as ebb and flow, wind, sun, rain and lightning, but also with boulders, branches, earth, clay and driftwood. The artists collected these natural materials and rearranged them in the landscape. Many of the resulting works recall ancient symbols such as the spiral, circle and line. A country hike can be a work of art to a land artist. Richard Long (1945), for instance, went on a four-day walk along all the river beds inside a circle which he had plotted beforehand. All these Land Art activities are documented in photographs, films and maps. Occasionally an entire work was transferred to the museum, like Richard Long's **Stone Line**.

Richard Serra, **Spin Out**, 1972-73

Richard Serra (1939)

Richard Serra selected a site in the sculpture park for his work. A natural dell is marked by three huge steel plates. They are placed on their short ends and partly pushed into the sloping terrain. Due to their position and size, the plates dominate the space so strongly that a visitor standing in the middle has the sensation of a spiral movement which is simultaneously menacing and liberating.

Serra titled his centrifugal piece **Spin Out**. It was his first large-scale commission for a site-specific work. Serra's work is always about space, gravity and balance. He usually works with Cor-Ten steel. Plates, several feet high and wide and weighing thousand of kilos each, are generally juxtaposed or supported against a wall in such a way that they keep in balance. They are often slightly

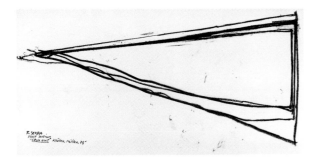

Richard Serra, **Plate Section Spin Out**, 1973

Richard Serra, **One**, 1987-88

askew, looking as though they might fall over at any moment. However, their own weight and the pressure they exert on each other that keeps them upright. As Serra puts it: 'I want to carry the effect of gravity in my pieces to absurdity.' This remarkable feat of balance is not his prime concern, though; more important is the circumstance that his works are made for a particular site or space. They stand out in their surroundings, their impact on the space so powerful that they affect and disrupt it, or introduce an unexpected tension. As a contrast with the closed, bowl-shaped site for **Spin Out**, Serra chose a spot at the back of the sculpture garden where four paths actually meet. The slightly tilted cylinder of solid forged steel (52 tons) is a concentration of material, mass and weight.

Mario Merz, **Igloo**, 1982

Mario Merz, **Prehistoric Wind from the Frozen Mountains**, 1962-78

Arte Povera

Partly as a reaction to the uniformity and technical perfection of the Minimal Art, a number of Italian artists turned to natural, fragile and perishable materials such as stone, twigs, wax, wood and textiles. They use this wide range of materials in a natural, sensitive manner. Their work was given the poetic name of 'Arte Povera', (poor art). 'Poor' not merely because simple materials were employed, but more particularly as opposed to the theoretical art of other movements of this period (Minimal Art, Conceptual Art). Arte Povera was more than an artistic rebellion; it was sparked off by a feeling of uneasiness about society. Man's broken relationship with nature and his isolated position in his culture are important themes. Many Arte Povera artists duly sought links with the culture of Classical Antiquity, the

Middle Ages and the Renaissance, eras in which man, art and science were still embedded in a larger, organic whole.

The Kröller-Müller museum has a unique collection of Arte Povera, with work by Anselmo, Fabro, Kounellis, Merz, Paolini, Pascali, Penone, Pistoletto and Zorio.

Mario Merz (1925) is the senior representative of Arte Povera. As well as natural resources - clay, twigs, plaster, wax, soil and stone - he uses modern materials like neon, glass and aluminium, which he combines and contrasts. In **Prehistoric Wind from the Frozen Mountains** a shaft of neon light penetrates a volcanic mountain like a lance. Numbers glow in the tightly bundled twigs at the foot of the mountain.

Gilberto Zorio, **Star**, 1977-87

Giulio Paolini, **Early Dynastic**, 1976

Jannis Kounellis, **Senza Titolo**, 1967

The digits - 1, 1, 2, 3, 5 - are the first numbers in the Fibonacci series. To Merz, this endless mathematical series in which each number is the sum of the two preceding ones and which has no zero, symbolizes growth processes. The Fibonacci series occurs in many of his works. So does the igloo, which Merz calls a 'mythical hut' and regards as archetypal of the human dwelling: a temporary home for the nomad roaming the world, not taking possession of things so that things do not take possession of him.

The work of **Jannis Kounellis** (1936) invariably exemplifies a contrast between nature and culture. In **Senza Titolo** he confronts what he sees as the technical, cold culture of our times with nature by making cactuses sprout from a closed, grey iron case.

Nature is the prime source and medium for **Giuseppe Penone** (1947). All his works are pervaded with memories of the forest, of trees. The tree as a symbol for everything that vegetation can mean to people: growth, fertility, shade, beauty and shelter. In **Otterlo Beech**, a bronze beech is integrated almost imperceptibly into an avenue of beeches in the wood, on the spot where a beech was missing. In the roots at the foot of the tree and in the leaves on the branches the vague impression of a human figure can be discerned. Exposed to the rain, wind and sun, the tree's bronze skin has taken on the colour of the surrounding tree-trunks.

Luciano Fabro (1936) combines forms and materials in such a way that they acquire a new, unexpected meaning. For his fairy-like piece

Giovanni Anselmo, **Panorama with Hand Pointing at it**, 1982

Giuseppe Penone, **Otterlo Beech**, 1987-88

called **The Two Faces of the Sky**, he suspended a large chunk of precious sky-blue marble in a net of steel cables between the trees. The face of the stone is polished smooth, looking like a picture of the transparent sky on a sunny day; the back is rough and unworked. This double-faced sky, like a tangible piece of sky, stirs the imagination.

Michelangelo Pistoletto, **Venus of the Rags**, 1967-82

Luciano Fabro, **The Two Faces of the Sky**, 1986

Fontana, Beuys, Nauman and Graham

It is not easy to pigeonhole the work of Lucio Fontana, Joseph Beuys, Bruce Nauman and Dan Graham. Their unconventional pieces rank today among the classics of modern sculpture.

Lucio Fontana (1899-1968) was fascinated by space. Not just physical, concrete space, but cosmic space too; space as a philosophical concept. This accounts for the title he gave to many of his works: **Concetto Spaziale**, spatial concept.

'If any one of my discoveries is important, it is the 'hole'. By 'hole' I mean going further than the limits of the framed canvas and being free in this notion of art.'

Bruce Nauman, **Untitled**, 1978

Bruce Nauman (1941) addresses space too, space as physical and psychic experience. In his performances, videos, drawings and sculptures he creates oppressive situations which induce sensations of fear, uncertainty and claustrophobia. **Untitled** (1978), consisting of three fibreglass rings, refers to Henry Moore's nightmarish tunnel drawings of crowds sheltering from air-raids in the London Underground during World War Two.

'I react emotionally and physically to the idea of being underground in a tunnel. It doesn't matter whether you're in a subway or not; but once you're down there you realize that you're ten metres underground. The idea of an enormous amount of earth above your head is very important.'

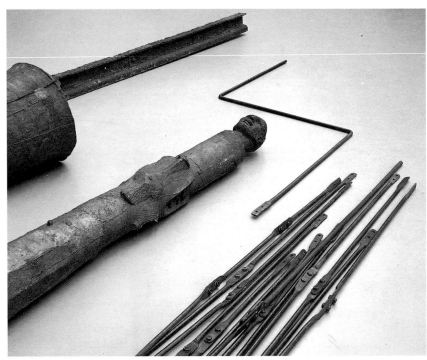

Joseph Beuys, **Secretion-cosmic-coming**, 1959

Joseph Beuys, **Tramstop**, 1976

Joseph Beuys (1921-1986) was undoubtedly the most influential and outstanding artist in Germany at the end of the last century. His ideas and his works, which brought anthroposophy, science, biology, economics and politics into the realm of art, and also his conviction that art and life are indissolubly linked and that everybody possesses the creative potential to be an artist, had a profound influence on art.

'Ideas move through people, whereas they freeze in artworks, and in the end are left behind.'
'What can be the point of art if not the humanitarian issue, if it cannot provide something that is substantially indispensable to mankind.'

Dan Graham, **Two Adjacent Pavilions**, 1978-81

The entire œuvre of **Dan Graham** (1942) centres
on the relationship between the beholder and the
object, between seeing and being seen. Through
video, film, photography, pavilions and models he
confronts the viewer with himself. For that reason
the mirror and reflection play a significant role in
his work.

'Since glass itself reflects, the mirror image
reflects a beholder who is looking, and also the
special interior or exterior space behind him in the
image of the space in which he is looking.'

Mendes da Costa, **Monument to Christiaan de Wet**, 1915-16

André Volten, **Column**, 1968

Carel Visser, **Cube and its Piling Up**, 1967

Dutch sculpture

Another salient aspect of the museum's collection is Dutch sculpture. Interestingly, Mrs. Kröller herself had commissioned a number of Dutch sculptors to provide monuments for distinctive spots in the Hoge Veluwe. In the twenties she also assembled a collection of figurines, mostly by Dutch sculptors.

For a long time Dutch sculpture served a primarily functional purpose. Besides a few monuments, statues and decorations were made before the years prior before World War Two to embellish the architecture of buildings and bridges (Raedecker, Mendes da Costa, Krop). This sculpture was characterized by closed and stylized forms and the use of different kinds of stone.

Not until around 1950, following a period in which a large number of war memorials were produced,

did sculpture develop in a more autonomous direction. Notable sculptors of this period were Wessel Couzijn, André Volten and Carel Visser, who at first were influenced by Gonzalez, Lipchitz and Zadkine but were also inspired by the geometrical abstractions of the Constructivists. In the sixties these artists struck out in a new

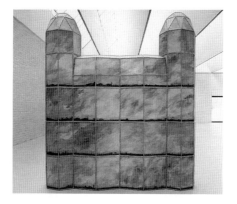

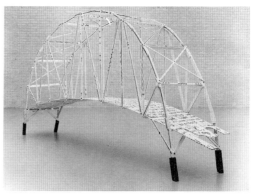

Michiel Schierbeek, **Fin de siècle**, 1985

Arno van der Mark, **The library**, 1988

Harald Vlugt, **Landshape**, 1985

Henk Visch, **Untitled**, 1980

Gerrit van Bakel, **Rain Cart**, 1982-83

Fortuyn/O'Brien, **The twenty-four men in white**, 1988

direction, Visser (1928) taking the cube as the basis for his investigation of symmetry, double forms and shifting planes. Volten (1925-2002), too, was intrigued by geometric abstraction during this period, producing granite cubes and aluminium cylinders in which weight, size and optical shifts played a part.

At the beginning of 1980, Dutch sculpture expanded enormously. Sculptors moved into the territory of painting, photography, the stage set, architecture and design. The borders between the various disciplines became blurred. A free, associative use of material generated a wide variety of pieces, some with a graceful, elegant character, others extremely complex and layered.

Besides the relationship with nature and the landscape, the use of themes from art history characterises a lot of Dutch sculpture.

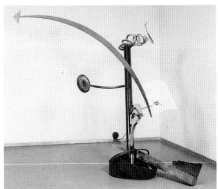

Pjotr Müller, **Nuraghe**, 1983

David van de Kop, **07.30 a.m.**, 1985

Marc Ruygrok, **Ambassadors**, 1985

Alexander Schabracq, **Monumental Assemblage with Arrow**, 1983

Niek Kemps, **The Birth of Venus**, 1983

Leo Vroegindeweij, **Untitled**, 1982

The beholder's role is changing too; one is expected to react sensitively tó, and participate actively in the sculptural experience. As well as bizarre, multi-coloured pieces, restrained, contemplative works are also made. Working methods range from sound craftsmanship to airy assemblages of a wide variety of materials.

Marta Pan, Project for sculpture garden with **Floating Sculpture Otterlo**, 1960-61 and **Cloud Shepherd** of Jean Arp, 1953

A walk through the sculpture garden

Around 1955 the then director of the Kröller-Müller Museum Professor A.M. Hammacher, in collaboration with the landscape architect Professor J.T.P. Bijhouwer, designed a garden in which sculptures could be displayed in the woods behind the museum. It was the first permanent sculpture garden designed especially for a museum's sculpture collection.

Over the years this garden has increased in size. In 2002 it was enlarged still further by the addition of an area with new paths, open spaces, extensive stretches of woodland and a large space for events, exhibitions and other activities. With this new extension, designed by landscape architect Adriaan Geuze of West 8, the garden now covers an area of 25 hectares.

Access is through the museum foyer. The two large lawns remind one of spacious sculpture galleries with shrubbery and trees for walls and the sky for a ceiling. The first section was designed in 1961 by Marta Pan: the lake, the floating sculpture, the path and the lawn. It was the first time that an artist created a place of her own in the park. Floating on the lake is an abstract polyester sculpture whose upper and lower sections move independently in the wind.

There is also space in Marta Pan's design for Arp's **Cloud Shepherd** and Aeschbacher's **Figure 1**. Aeschbacher's severely vertical sculpture contrasts with the horizontal character of Marta Pan's piece. Displayed on the large adjacent lawn are works by Rodin, Bourdelle, Lipchitz, Permeke, Maillol, Wotruba, Couzijn and Richmond. They all

Arturo Martini, **Judith en Holofernes**, 1932-33

Evert Strobos, **Palisade**, 1973

represent human figures whose various attitudes express an emotion or an idea, or tell a story. Returning to the entrance towards the Rietveld pavilion, you will encounter a colourful early piece by Christo, 56 stacked oil-drums.
In and around the Rietveld pavilion are works by Hepworth (see p. 43). Rietveld's pavilion, designed in 1955 for the Sonsbeek exhibition in Arnhem, was rebuilt in the park ten years later (see p. 10). In a clearing a little further on is a striking work by Etienne-Martin. **Demure no. 3** represents a dwelling, a safe haven. A kind of revolving chair in the centre is surrounded by bizarre forms with defensive and protecting hands.
Hewn from a single stone, Martini's impressive sculpture, a little further on, re-tells the dramatic bible story of **Judith and Holofernes**. Follow the

path to the right to see sculptures by Mastroianni, Paolozzi and Penalba.
Carry on along this path and you will encounter more Hepworth bronzes. Turn right when you reach the large field with Serra's **Spin Out** (see p. 52). Carry on towards a flight of wooden steps leading to an extremely large work by Van de Wint. Entitled **View, 2002**, it is made of Cor-Ten steel and dominates the hill with its enormous arched steel plates, which are reminiscent of a plant's huge leaves.
On the ridge of 'French Hill' is Chen Zhen's piece, a reference to the cultural revolution in China. Continuing your walk, you will arrive at a new flight of descending steps, flanked by Japanese and oriental steles and sculptures. These funerary statues come from Helene Kröller-Müller's collection.

Jean Dubuffet, **Jardin d'Email**, 1972-73

Per Kirkeby, **Brick Sculpture for Kröller-Müller**, 1988

Ian Hamilton Finlay, **Five Columns for the Kröller-Müller**, 1980-82

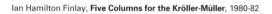

Shirazeh Houshiary, **Angel with Ten Thousand Wings**, 1988

Ulrich Rückriem, **Untitled**, 1988

The large constructions down in the field are by Snelson (see p. 46), Volten and Visser (see p. 63). Here, too, are Rogge's tents. Behind the rhododendrons you will find another large-scale work by Van de Wint, **Beeld 7**, an enigmatic sculpture consisting of horizontal and vertical bars, a triple fence to which, despite its open character, there is no admittance. In the adjoining field are Dodeigne's **Man and Woman**, **43 Roaring Forty** by Andre, Merz' **Igloo** (see p. 54) and **Concetto Spaziale** by Fontana (see p. 59).

Finlay's work is not easy to find: it is near Merz' **Igloo**, hidden among the rhododendrons.

In Finlay's arrangement the trees stand as columns on five stone pedestals carved with the names Rousseau, Corot, Robespierre, Michelet and Lycurgus. In this tranquil spot Finlay takes us back in time to the French Revolution. His theme is order and chaos in history.

Take the path to the left to see sculptures by Van der Weide, Strobos, and Visser. Dubuffet's **Jardin d'Émail** looms up at the end of the path. The enormous installation was designed especially for this site. Behind high white walls, surrounded by vegetation, is a dazzlingly white artificial landscape: a garden within a garden. The lively black lines give it the air of a three-dimensional painting. Dubuffet called this type of sculpture 'peinture monumentée'. He was often inspired by drawings by children or the mentally ill.

Behind the **Jardin d'Émail** begins the avenue of beeches leading to the lovely wooded area that was added to the sculpture garden in 2002. Here, in the midst of varied vegetation, stand a number

R.W. van de Wint, **Sculpture 7**

Sjoerd Buisman, **Phyllotaxis**, 1987

Jan van Munster, **+ –**, 1987-88

Hermann Maier Neustadt, **WD-Spiral Part One Cinema**, 2001

Chen Zhen, **Resonance**, 1994-99

of fascinating sculptures, each of which enters into a relationship with its natural surroundings. Halfway down the avenue, on the right, is Penone's intriguing bronze, **Otterlo Beech** (see p. 56). Dotted around the woodland on the left are the following sculptures: **Angel with Ten Thousand Wings** by Houshiary, **18 Lying Wooden Men** by Claasen and LeWitt's **Six-Sided Tower**. Turn right off the beech avenue at Raedecker's **Antlers** and halfway along the path you will encounter Volten's **Sculpture in Four Parts** and, at the end of the path on the left, Fabro's blue marble sculpture, suspended between two trees like a tangible piece of sky: **The Two Faces of the Sky** (p. 57). Bear right to see, rearing up against French Hill, Maier Neustadt's **Cinema**, a large object in which you can sit and contemplate the woods. Turning left after Fabro's work will bring you to a colossal

mass of steel forged into a cylinder, Serra's **One** (see p. 53). It may be seen as a companion to his earlier **Spin Out** on the other side of the park. Follow this path to the left to spy sculptures by Kirkeby, Buisman, U-Fan Lee and Van Munster hiding in the wood. Piet Hein Eek's work makes interesting use of waste material; it was designed as a gatehouse to the sculpture garden. Walk past it to leave the garden through Rückriem's stone gate, two huge blocks of granite split horizontally and vertically. But if you stroll back to the museum through the garden you could end your walk where Stanley Brouwn began one of his on December 23 1984. Here and there you will see Brouwn's mysterious white signs reading **starting-point of a distance of ... steps walked by Stanley Brouwn**, an invitation, repeated several times by the artist, to reflect on a real or imaginary walk.

The following reproduced works came from the collection
Visser: Christo, Empaquetage, 1961; Sol LeWitt, 6 Part Piece,
1968; Carl Andre, Henge on Threshold, 1960, Square piece,
1967, 35 Timber Row, 1968

Photocredits:
F. André de La Porte
Alexander van de Berge
J. Brokerhof
Tom Haartsen
Elize Heuker of Hoek
Wouter van Heusden
J. Holtman
Cary Markerink
Arie Melissen
Victor E. Nieuwenhuijs
Hans Sibbelee
Jan en Fridtjof Versnel
Cor van Weele

Administration:
Margriet Vooren

Printed:
Lecturis BV, Eindhoven

Compiled and edited by:
Angeline Bremer-Cox en Rieja Brouns

Edited by:
Angeline Bremer-Cox

Translation: Ruth Koenig, Buren

ISBN
90-74453-30-9